SHOCK ZONE™
TRUE SURVIVAL STORIES

SuRVIVING ACCIDENTS and CRASHES

MARCIA AMIDON LUSTED

Lerner Publications Company • Minneapolis

Cover photo: Rescuers saved all 155 people on board a US Airways flight that made an emergency landing in the Hudson River in New York in 2009.

Copyright © 2014 by
Lerner Publishing Group, Inc.

All rights reserved. International
copyright secured. No part of this book
may be reproduced, stored in a retrieval
system, or transmitted in any form or by any
means—electronic, mechanical, photocopying,
recording, or otherwise—without the prior
written permission of Lerner Publishing Group,
Inc., except for the inclusion of brief quotations in an
acknowledged review.

Lerner Publications Company
A division of Lerner Publishing Group, Inc.
241 First Avenue North
Minneapolis, MN 55401 USA

For reading levels and more information, look up this title at
www.lernerbooks.com

Library of Congress Cataloging-in-Publication Data

Lusted, Marcia Amidon.
    Surviving accidents and crashes / by Marcia Amidon Lusted.
      pages   cm. — (Shockzone. True survival stories)
    Includes index.
    ISBN 978–1–4677–1439–6 (lib. bdg. : alk. paper)
    ISBN 978–1–4677–2510–1 (eBook)
    1. Survival—Juvenile literature. 2. Accident victims—Juvenile literature. I. Title.
  GF86.L87 2014
  613.6'9—dc23   2013025292

Manufactured in the United States of America
1 — PC — 12/31/13

TABLE OF CONTENTS

SURVIVING THE UNEXPECTED

The lights in the airplane dim. You look out the window as the plane goes into a steep dive. You're knocked around violently in your seat. **What do you do?**

People in cars, buses, trains, and airplanes get into crashes every day. Accidents strike in dangerous places, such as underground mines and wells. Some of these disasters look as though no one could have possibly survived them. Cars can end up crumpled like aluminum foil. Planes can burst into flames when they crash into the ground. Mine collapses drop tons of rocks on workers' heads. But people have survived some of the most terrible crashes and accidents. Their stories are about bravery, strength, and luck. They can help us learn how we could survive such frightening events.

Imagine yourself in one of these disasters. What would you do? How would you react? Could you survive?

Car crashes take people's lives every day, but many others survive these grisly wrecks.

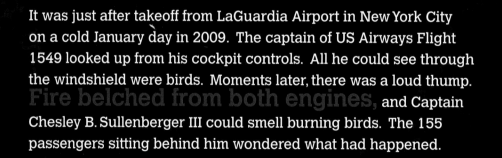

It was just after takeoff from LaGuardia Airport in New York City on a cold January day in 2009. The captain of US Airways Flight 1549 looked up from his cockpit controls. All he could see through the windshield were birds. Moments later, there was a loud thump. Fire belched from both engines, and Captain Chesley B. Sullenberger III could smell burning birds. The 155 passengers sitting behind him wondered what had happened.

The engines failed, and the plane was unable to climb higher. Captain Sullenberger knew that he wouldn't be able to make it back to the airport. One of the copilots radioed the airport and said, "We can't do it. We're gonna end up in the Hudson [River]." Captain Sullenberger knew that the best chance to keep his passengers and crew safe was to land the plane near boats in the river. Nearby freeways were filled with cars. It was safer to land on the water. Landing near boats would help rescuers get to the

The gathered crowd cheered each time a miner emerged from the rescue capsule.

ALONE IN THE DARK

Thanks to their experience with spacecraft, experts from the National Aeronautics and Space Administration (NASA) know what it's like to be trapped in a small space for months at a time. Because of this, the US space agency sent one of its doctors to help monitor the thirty-three miners while they were trapped. The doctor knew what health conditions the miners were probably suffering from because of their tiny amounts of food and lack of sunlight. He helped the rescue team decide what foods and medicines should be sent down to the trapped men. Other NASA experts helped design the *Fenix 2* capsule.

The capsule was only 21 inches (53 centimeters) across and 6.5 feet (2 m) high, just big enough to hold one man. It would bring the trapped men back to the surface, one at a time.

Finally, sixty-nine days after the accident, the first miner was hauled up to the surface. When he stepped out of the capsule, his nine-year-old son burst into tears and hugged him. By the end of the day, all thirty-three men had been rescued. As he reached the surface, miner Jorge Galleguillos said, "Thank you for believing that we were alive."

A Fatal Parade

"It was a horrible accident to watch happen right in front of me," a witness later said. "I just saw the people on the semi-truck's trailer panic, and many started to jump off the trailer. But it was too late for many of them."

The scene was a Veteran's Day parade in Midland, Texas, in 2012. A flatbed truck carrying a float filled with wounded veterans was creeping across railroad tracks. They were on their way to a banquet. Suddenly, the crossing gates began to lower. A freight train with its horn blaring was heading right for the float. Some of the people riding on the float were able to jump off in time. But

banquet = a special meal, often held in someone's honor

then the train hit the flatbed truck. Witnesses heard "a low whoosh and a thunderous crack."

Patricia Howle was in her car behind the parade float. "My daughter said, 'Momma, the train is coming!'" Howle said. "People were jumping off, trying to get off that trailer and the truck was still rolling. . . . I covered my face. I didn't want to see." A soldier named Joshua Michael managed to push his wife off the float. He didn't have time to save himself. A friend later told reporters, "His first instinct was to get her out of harm's way."

Four people riding on the float were killed that day, and seventeen others were injured. Veteran heroes like Joshua Michael helped prevent even greater tragedy. They remembered their battlefield training and saved the lives of others.

Investigators attempted to re-create the circumstances of the crash to understand how the accident happened.

HURTLING TOWARD THE GROUND

"The pilot tried to bring the plane back up," said Millie Furlong. "He started to turn right ... then the plane went into the embankment. I saw the grass and knew we were going to crash. It was very quick."

embankment = a mound of earth or stone built to control floods

It was September 2007. Furlong was one of 130 passengers aboard Flight OG269, heading for the resort island of Phuket in Thailand. The plane crashed while trying to land in heavy rain and wind. As soon as the plane came to rest, it burst into flames. Furlong remembers the passenger compartment filling with heavy smoke. "There were flames everywhere and people burning," she said. Most of the passengers seated in the front of the plane died on impact. The rest were trapped by smoke and flames.

Then one passenger took action to save everyone. A man seated behind Furlong started kicking at the emergency exit door, which was stuck shut. "You could hear his foot hitting the door as he was kicking it," she remembered. He kept kicking and kicking it until it began to open. "At first it was just a crack," she said. "It was quite difficult to make it peel back. And then finally it did, at the last second, right before everybody passed out." She added, "If it hadn't opened we would have died. It was dark and smoky. I felt like I was going to pass out."

Forty-one passengers survived. Amazingly, Furlong had only suffered a few cuts.

TOXIC CHEMICALS

One of the greatest dangers in a plane crash is something people don't always think of. As various parts of the airplane burn, they release toxic fumes and chemicals. These aren't just dangerous to passengers. They may also cause lasting health effects for rescuers who breathe them.

The crash ripped the airliner to shreds.

Trapped in a Well

"I was scared, panicked," remembered eighteen-year-old Reba Cissy McClure. "I didn't know what to do. I just ran in and called the police. They were there within three minutes, but it felt like a lifetime." McClure's eighteen-month-old baby, Jessica, had just fallen down the 8-inch (20 cm) opening of an abandoned well shaft. The shaft was in the backyard of McClure's aunt's home in Midland, Texas. It was October 14, 1987.

B. J. Hall was the first police officer on the scene. "I went over and looked down the hole, but I couldn't see anything," Hall said. "I called the baby's name three or four times and didn't hear anything. Finally I got a cry in response."

Rescuers tried many different methods to get Jessica out, including using machines to dig out the well. Millions of people watched on television as rescuers worked day and night to reach her. They dug a hole next to the well, then dug sideways into the well. Fifty-eight hours after she fell in, Jessica was finally pulled out of the well. She was covered with dirt and bruises, and one of her toes had gangrene from being wedged in the shaft. She still has a scar where a pipe inside the well rubbed against her forehead. Jessica, who today has no memory of being inside the shaft for so long, is proud of her scars. "I have them because I survived," she says.

gangrene = the death of body tissue, sometimes caused by blocked blood circulation

Despite severe injuries, Jessica survived for more than fifty hours in the well.

Alone in the Jungle

"My mother said very calmly: 'That is the end, it's all over.' Those were the last words I ever heard from her." This is how Juliane Koepcke described the last moments on board a flight to Peru on Christmas Eve 1971. Some of the passengers had just seen a bright light come out of an engine. Then the plane jolted and went into a nosedive. It was pitch-black. Passengers were screaming. The next thing she knew, seventeen-year-old Koepcke was outside the plane. She was falling through the air, still strapped into her seat. She fell 10,000 feet (3,000 m) before disappearing into the thick jungle canopy.

"I could see the canopy of the jungle spinning towards me," Koepcke said. "Then I lost consciousness and remember nothing of the impact. Later I learned that the plane had broken into pieces about two miles (3 kilometers) above the ground." The dense branches of the jungle slowed her fall and allowed her to survive. But Koepcke had broken her collarbone in the crash and torn a ligament in one knee. She had several deep cuts on her arms and legs. One of the sandals she had been wearing was lost in the fall. She had also lost her glasses.

She got out of her seat and went looking for help. Koepcke used her sandal to feel the ground in front of her because she couldn't see well. As she moved through the jungle, she avoided snakes and insects. Several times she found the bodies of other passengers from her flight. Koepcke kept moving through the jungle. There was no sign of civilization. Her chances of survival were not looking good.

The harsh Amazon rain forest makes survival difficult—especially when you are alone.

WHAT ARE THE SAFEST SEATS IN AN AIRPLANE DURING A CRASH?

If you're taking an airplane trip, where is the safest part of the plane to be seated in case of a crash? Here are the chances of survival in a crash when seated in different areas of the aircraft.

49%

56%

56%

69%

After ten days alone in the jungle, Koepcke was exhausted and starving. She was following a stream because walking in the water with one bare foot seemed safer than the jungle floor. Finally, she came to a hut where she found a container of gasoline. "I had a wound on my upper right arm," she said. "It was infested with maggots. I remembered our dog had the same infection and my father had put kerosene in it, so I sucked the gasoline out and put it into the wound." It worked. The gasoline drove the maggots out. She decided to stay overnight in the hut.

maggots =
wormlike larva
that grow into flies

The next morning, Koepcke heard voices. Several local lumberjacks found her. They gave her food and took her back to civilization. Her father, who had not been on the plane, was overjoyed to discover she was alive. Several days passed before her mother's body was found in the jungle. Her mother had apparently survived the crash, but she had been so badly injured that she died soon after.

As the only survivor of the crash, Koepcke became known as the miracle girl. She received hundreds of letters from people she didn't even know. Her incredible story of survival touched people from around the world.

Koepcke later moved to Germany and became a biologist.

Swim or Die

It was July of 2011. Michael Trapp was happily piloting his small Cessna airplane over Lake Huron near Michigan. There was no land in sight. Suddenly the engine noise changed, and the airplane began to lose power. It was unable to stay aloft. Trapp radioed a nearby airport. "I'm over the water, and my engine is having trouble," he said. Then suddenly he shouted, "I'm going into the drink!"

The tail of the airplane hit the water first. The plane somersaulted, and the windshield blew inward. Water quickly filled the cockpit. Trapp managed to unbuckle his safety harness and swim out of the open door. He held onto the plane's tail as long as he could. But in less than a minute, the plane sank from sight in the deep waters of Lake Huron.

Trapp began swimming and treading water to stay alive. He tried making a flotation device from his pants, but it nearly strangled him. As the sun set, he waited for rescue. He finally realized no one was coming that night. He would have to hold out until the next day.

By morning he was exhausted. But he managed to keep his head above water. He tried to use the sun's reflection off his credit card to attract the attention of planes. When boats passed by at a distance, he screamed and yelled, but no one heard him. He was almost run over by a huge freight ship. Trapp was extremely cold and tired. But he knew there were only two choices: swim or die.

Finally, as he neared the end of his strength, Trapp saw a boat not far off. On the boat, Dean Petitpren spotted Trapp. "He had his socks off, and he was waving the socks over his head," Petitpren said. "It looked like he was going to drown." It had been eighteen hours since the crash. The crew pulled Trapp onto the boat and wrapped him in a blanket. "I enjoy my life," he said later. "I have fun. I'm just not ready to give it all up yet."

Trapp described his survival story to reporters in the hospital after his rescue.

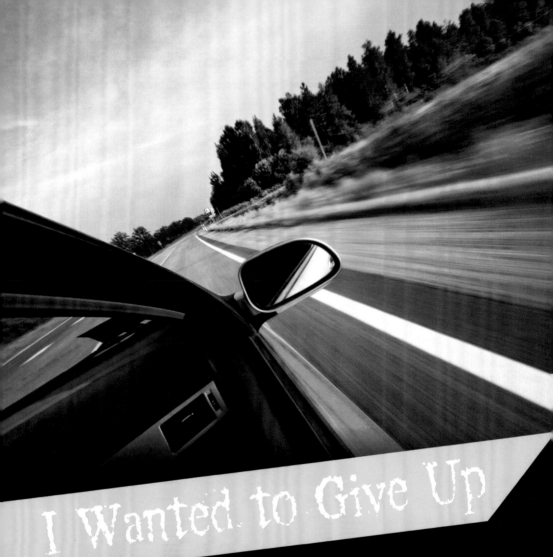

I Wanted to Give Up

"The water was so cold it woke me up, and all I remember is everybody in the car talking about death," eighteen-year-old Brian Henry said. "Everybody was talking about 'We about to die, we about to die.' When I heard that, I wanted to give up, but I couldn't."

Henry was one of eight teens who had crammed into a sport utility vehicle (SUV) early on a Sunday morning in March 2013. He remembered that the SUV's driver, nineteen-year-old Alexis Cayson, seemed to be driving recklessly. Henry was sitting beside her in

He remembers pleading with her to slow down. But she sped up when she came to a part of the road known in Warren, Ohio, as Dead Man's Curve. "The car had jerked out of control," Henry said. "I don't know if she did it on purpose, or how fast she was going."

The SUV flew off the road and into a pond. Henry blacked out. When he came to his senses, he found himself upside down in the pond. The car was quickly filling with water. One of his friends yelled to him to break the windows. Henry threw his elbow into the window seven times before it shattered. But he could only get partway out of the SUV. Seat belts were wrapped around his legs. Henry reached for the car's muffler to pull himself out and burned his fingers on the hot metal.

The pond they crashed into was small, but being trapped in the SUV threatened the teens' lives.

TEENS AND CAR CRASHES

Car crashes are the most common cause of death for people between the ages of thirteen and nineteen. Most of these deaths are preventable. People who text or talk on their phones while driving have a much higher accident rate. So do people who speed. And more than half of teens who die in car crashes aren't wearing seat belts. The best way to survive a car accident is to not get into one in the first place. Drive safely and without distractions to maximize your chances of survival.

Finally, Henry managed to free his legs and swim away. As soon as he broke the surface, he ran to get help. Another boy, Asher, also escaped and joined Henry in looking for help. Two cars passed them by as they waved frantically. Finally, they found a house and banged on the door.

The homeowner was startled but recognized one of the boys and soon came to help.

When cars begin to slip beneath the water, passengers often have only seconds to escape.

"They were so scared," she remembered. "They were shaking and so cold." Asher later told police that it felt like the SUV was going 80 miles (129 km) per hour right before the crash. It was later discovered that the SUV was stolen, and the driver did not have a license. Sadly, none of the other teens in the SUV survived. Five had drowned in the car, and the sixth had been thrown from the car during the crash and was crushed beneath it.

Henry had been unable to stop the crash from happening. But breaking the window meant the difference between life and death during the tragic accident.

Friends of the victims left memorials at the site of the accident.

10 Tips for Surviving a Plane Crash

1. When you take your seat on the plane, find the two exits
    closest to you. Count the rows of seats between you and those
    exits. If the plane is filled with smoke, you may have to feel
    your way along rows of seats to the exits.

2. Always wear long pants, a long-sleeved shirt, and shoes with
    closed toes. They can help protect you from flying debris.

3. If the plane is going to crash, get into crash position: cross
    your hands on the seat in front of you, and lean your head
    against them. Tuck your feet under your seat.

4. Always pay attention to the instructions the flight attendants give you before you take off. Every plane is different, and they'll give you valuable information.

5. If there's a fire while the plane is on the ground, stay low and get out of the plane as quickly as possible to avoid toxic smoke.

6. Move quickly. Statistics show that if you can get out of the plane within ninety seconds, you're more likely to survive.

7. Read the safety card in the pocket of your seat.

8. Once you get out of the plane, get as far away from it as possible in case of an explosion.

9. When you leave the plane, don't try to take any of your carry-on luggage with you.

10. If you land on water, don't inflate your life vest until you get out of the plane. It makes it harder to move.

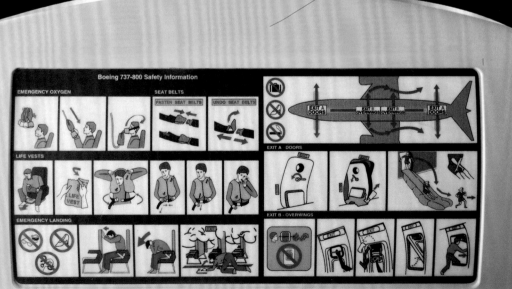

Bryant, Charles W. "How to Survive a Plane Crash"
http://www.howstuffworks.com/how-to-survive-a-plane-crash.htm
Did you know that more than 90 percent of US airplane crash victims between
1980 and 2000 survived? Learn this and other interesting facts in this article.

Emergency Mine Rescue
http://www.pbs.org/wgbh/nova/tech/emergency-mine-rescue.html
Find information, photos, interviews, and video from the PBS show *Nova*
about the incredible Chile mine rescue operation.

Nice, Karim. "How Crash Testing Works"
http://auto.howstuffworks.com/car-driving-safety/accidents-hazardous-
conditions/crash-test.htm
This article explains how companies test their cars to make them safer. It
also includes slow-motion videos of these amazing tests.

Operation Lifesaver
http://oli.org/index.php
This website contains tons of videos and activities to get you up to speed on
railroad safety. It also has handy tips and stats about the railroad industry.

Plane Crash in the Hudson River
http://www.time.com/time/photogallery/0,29307,1872244,00.html
This website from *Time* magazine features stunning photos from the
Hudson River plane rescue.

Ten Crashes That Changed Airplane History
http://www.popularmechanics.com/technology/aviation/crashes/
10-airplane-crashes-that-changed-aviation#slide-1
This slide show includes pictures and descriptions of ten major airplane
crashes that changed the way planes are built and pilots are trained.

Woods, Michael, and Mary B. Woods. *Disasters Up Close: Air Disasters.*
Minneapolis: Lerner Publications Company, 2007.
Check out this book for an in-depth look at what causes plane crashes, the
ways first responders react to them, and tons of info about plane safety.

LERNER

SOURCE

Expand learning beyond the printed book. Download free, complementary
educational resources for this book from our website, www.lerneresource.com.

6 Matthew L. Wald and Al Baker, "1549 to Tower: 'We're Gonna End Up in the Hudson,'" New York Times, January 17, 2009, http://www.nytimes.com/2009/01/18/nyregion/18plane.html?_r=3&.

7 "Airplane Crash-lands into Hudson River; All Aboard Reported Safe," CNN, January 15, 2009, http://www.cnn.com/2009/US/01/15/new.york.plane.crash/index.html.

7 "US Airways Flight 1549 Crew Receive Prestigious Guild of Air Pilots and Air Navigators Award," The Guild of Air Pilots and Navigators, January 22, 2009, http://www.gapan.org/ruth-documents/Masters%20Medal%20%20Press%20Release.pdf.

8 "Emergency Mine Rescue," PBS, 2010, http://www.pbs.org/wgbh/nova/tech/emergency-mine-rescue.html.

9 "Ten Biggest Stories of 2010," CNN, December 31, 2010, http://transcripts.cnn.com/TRANSCRIPTS/1012/31/cnr.02.html.

10 "Emergency Mine Rescue."

11 "Quotes from Chile's Dramatic Mine Rescue," Sydney Morning Herald, October 14, 2010, http://www.smh.com.au/world/quotes-from-chiles-dramatic-mine-rescue-20101014-16kxn.html.

12 Juan Carlos Llorca, "Texas Parade Honoring War Heroes Ends in Tragedy," Associated Press, November 16, 2012, http://bigstory.ap.org/article/deadly-train-parade-float-crash-texas-probed.

13 Ibid.

13 Whitney Harding, "Eyewitness Account from Train Accident 11/15/12," CBS7 News (West Texas), n.d., http://www.cbs7kosa.com/news/details.asp?ID=38998.

13 "Texas Parada Honoring War Heroes Ends in Tragedy."

14 "B.C. Woman Survives Thai Plane Crash," Canada.com, September 17, 2007, http://www.canada.com/theprovince/story.html?id=ce27c153-fc44-4f9e-97ee-5ab3378279de&k=68101.

14 Thomas Fuller, "Survivors Recount Thai Plane Crash," New York Times, September 17, 2007, http://www.nytimes.com/2007/09/17/world/asia/17cnd-thai.html.

15 "B.C. Woman Survives Thai Plane Crash."

16 Lianne Hart and Anne Maier, "The Epic Rescue of Jessica McClure," People, November 2, 1987, http://www.people.com/people/archive/article/0,,20193651,00.html.

17 Simon Neville, "Baby Jessica at 25," Daily Mail, October 17, 2012, http://www.dailymail.co.uk/news/article-2218731/Jessica-Morales-Famous-toddler-rescued-1987-married-children.html.

18 "Juliane Koepcke: How I Survived a Plane Crash," BBC, March 23, 2012, http://www.bbc.co.uk/news/magazine-17476615.

20 Ibid.

22 Derek Burnett, "Mayday! One Man's Story of Surviving a Plane Crash," Reader's Digest, February 2012, http://www.rd.com/true-stories/survival/mayday/.

23 Ibid.

24 Kara Sutyak and Emily Valdez, "Crash Survivor: 'I Wanted to Give Up, But I Couldn't,'" Fox8 News (Cleveland), March 11, 2013, http://fox8.com/2013/03/11/crash-survivor-i-wanted-to-give-up-but-i-couldnt/.

25 "Driver in Ohio Crash that Left 6 Teens Dead Had No License," Fox News, March 12, 2013, http://www.foxnews.com/us/2013/03/12/driver-in-ohio-crash-that-left-6-teens-dead-had-no-license/.

27 Ibid.

INDEX

PHOTO ACKNOWLEDGMENTS

The images in this book are used with the permission of: © iStockphoto/Thinkstock, pp. 4–5; © Ververidis Vasilis/Shutterstock Images, p. 5; © Seth Wenig/AP Images, p. 6; © Steven Day/AP Images, p. 7; © Jorge Saenz/AP Images, pp. 8, 11; © Hector Retamal/AP Images, p. 9; © Chile's Presidency/AP Images, p. 10; © Juan Carlos Llorca/AP Images, p. 12; © James Durbin/Reporter-Telegram/AP Images, p. 13; © Aleksandar Mijatovic/Shutterstock Images, p. 14; © David Longstreath/AP Images, p. 15; © AP Images, pp. 16, 21; © J. P. Hearn/AP Images, p. 17; © Alexey Stiop/Shutterstock Images, p. 18; © Dr. Morley Read/Shutterstock Images, p. 19; © Red Line Editorial/VectorZilla/Shutterstock Images, p. 20; © Ed Darack/Science Faction/SuperStock, p. 22; © Jeff Schrier/The Saginaw News/AP Images, p. 23; © Nejron Photo/Shutterstock Images, p. 24; © Tony Dejak/AP Images, p. 25; © 1000 Words/Shutterstock Images, p. 26; © Scott R. Galvin/AP Images, p. 27; © photobank.ch/Shutterstock Images, p. 28; © Barone Firenze/Shutterstock Images, p. 29.
Front Cover: ERIC THAYER/REUTERS/Newscom.

Main body text set in Calvert MT Std Regular 11/16.
Typeface provided by Monotype Typography.